Claims *to* Fame
Fourteen Short Biographies

Book 2

Carol Einstein

Educators Publishing Service
Cambridge and Toronto

Cover and book design by Joyce Weston
Illustrations on pages 81 and 106 by Anne Lord

Educators Publishing Service
800.225.5750
www.epsbooks.com

Printed in U.S.A.
ISBN 0-8388-2375-0

4 5 6 7 8 VGP 09 08 07 06 05

To my husband, who encouraged and
helped me every step of the way.
With thanks and love,
C.S.E.

Contents

Acknowledgments

To those no longer here: Bernice Einstein, Recha Einstein-Weil, and Julie Weil.

To my colleagues, friends, and family: Joan Amron, Bonnie Tiburzi Caputo, Susanna Einstein, Maureen Farbstein, Aaron Kessler, Bonnie Long, and Charles Thompson. You were always willing to listen and to help. With special thanks to my skillful and understanding editor, Mary Troeger, who always catches my errors and clarifies my thoughts.

New York City

Dear Reader,

Before you start reading these stories, I want to tell you how I came to write this book. When I was your age, I always loved hearing family stories about the interesting things my grandmother and great aunts did when they were young. I also loved reading stories about real people who had lived before I was born. When I grew up and started working with children, many of my students said they wished there were more books telling about women who had lived long ago. Then my students told me they would like some of the stories to be about men, too, and about people living right now. So in this book you will find all of these kinds of stories.

I hope that you enjoy reading them and find these lives as interesting as I did.

Carol Einstein

Courtesy of Yahoo!

Jerry Yang
1968–

Jerry Yang, a **founder** of **Yahoo!,** turned his hobby of spending a lot of time on the World Wide Web into a successful business. He says that he is now doing exactly what he wants to be doing.

Jerry was born in Taiwan. When he was two, his father died. His mother, a professor of English and drama, raised him and his younger brother Ken. Because her sister lived in the United States, Jerry's mother decided to move there, too. The family settled in San Jose, California, when he was ten years old.

Jerry started school knowing only one English word—*shoe.* He says that at first he could not pay attention in class for very long, but soon he was doing quite well.

After high school, Jerry went to Stanford University to study engineering. One of his good friends there was David Filo, another engineering student. They set up a tiny office in a university trailer as a place to study. Both Jerry and Dave used the World Wide Web to get information. They spent a lot of time looking at the many different **sites.**

The World Wide Web was just beginning. Many people were putting all kinds of information on the Web, but it was not in any order. Jerry learned that there was no easy way to find the information he wanted. He had to look at everything. He decided to build himself a guide. He began by making little lists of **links** to his favorite Web sites. This made it faster to find what he wanted.

Dave was doing the same thing with his favorite sites. Soon they were passing links back and forth. They decided to combine them into a shared list.

Jerry and Dave e-mailed the Web address for their guide to a few friends, who thought the guide was very helpful. They began sending it to their friends. Soon many people were using it. The list became known as *David and Jerry's Guide to the World Wide Web.*

Before long the list became too big. Jerry and Dave decided to divide it into different categories or classes. Soon the lists of categories got too big, so they broke them into smaller ones. In this way Jerry and Dave developed the basic idea behind Yahoo!, and it has not changed much since then.

To let people know about new and interesting sites, they expanded their guide with short listings like "What's Cool." Their audience cheered every new item with encouraging e-mails, which also contained lots of helpful advice. Jerry believes that if they had not had this help, they couldn't have developed Yahoo!

One day in the fall of 1994, almost 100,000 people looked at their Web site. Jerry remembers, "That was the point at which we said, we've got to do something about this, or we're going to shut it down." The guide was taking up so much of their time that they almost did not eat, sleep, or study. So they decided to turn their hobby into a business.

Jerry and Dave needed money to develop Yahoo! They knew they would have to review more and more Web sites and put them in categories. They would have to hire people to do this work, and they would need more equipment. They quickly learned that many businesses were very eager to help them get started.

Since then Yahoo! has grown. Although now there are many different guides for finding information on the Web, Yahoo! is the oldest and remains one of the most popular. Jerry says, "I love what I'm doing. I don't even see it as a job."

· · · HELPFUL VOCABULARY · · ·

founder: the person who sets up or organizes something

Yahoo!: the first and most popular listing of what is on the World Wide Web

site: a particular place on the Web where one can find information

link: on a Web page, a place you click that takes you to another site

THINKING ABOUT WHAT YOU HAVE READ

1. Where was Jerry born?

_____

_____

2. Why was 1994 an important year for Jerry?

_____

_____

_____

3. Why did Jerry want to build a guide to the World Wide Web?

_____

_____

_____

4. How did their friends and the other people using their guide help Jerry and Dave?

_____

_____

_____

5. How did Jerry and Dave help each other?

_____

_____

_____

6. Why do you think Jerry likes his job so much?

_____

_____

7. What new sites would you like to see on the World Wide Web?

_____

_____

WORKING WITH WORDS

A **synonym** is a word that has the same or almost the same meaning as another word. *Large* is a synonym for *big*. In the story we learn that Jerry and Dave set up a *tiny* office. Can you think of three synonyms for *tiny*?

a _____ office

a _____ office

a _____ office

A **category** is a group or class of things. For example, the category of food includes milk, beef, apples, and so on. Jerry and Dave used categories to develop Yahoo! Try to list four items that belong in each category.

states

_____   _____

_____   _____

insects

_____   _____

_____   _____

jewelry

_____   _____

_____   _____

Sometimes words have more than one meaning. In the following sentences, the word in bold print has one meaning. Write what it is. Then write another meaning the word may have. Example: The family **settled** in San Jose, California. In the sentence, *settled* means to have gone to a place to stay and live *Settled* can also mean to have agreed on something.

Jerry's mother **raised** him and his brother.

_____

_____

Soon he was doing quite **well** in school.

_____

_____

David Filo was one of Jerry's **good** friends.

_____

_____

"What's **Cool**" is one of the listings on Yahoo!

_____

_____

One day in the **fall** of 1994, almost 100,000 people looked at their Web site.

_____

_____

WRITING SKILLS

Jerry Yang and Dave Filo are close friends. Write about a good friend you have. Think about where and when you met, what you like to do together, why you are friends, and any other things you want to include. Try to write at least three sentences.

_____

_____

_____

_____

Jerry liked to get suggestions from people about how to improve Yahoo! What suggestions do you have for Jerry?

_____

_____

_____

What do you like about using the World Wide Web? What don't you like?

_____

_____

_____

_____

How does a newspaper reporter get information for a story?

_____

_____

Courtesy of Library of Congress, LC-USZ62-97448

Elizabeth Cochrane
1867–1922

Elizabeth Cochrane, who signed her newspaper stories "Nellie Bly," was America's first **investigative** woman **reporter**. She became famous for the many daring things she did to get her stories.

Elizabeth was born in Cochran's Mills, Pennsylvania, in 1867. After her father died, her mother moved the family to Pittsburgh. Elizabeth wanted to write for newspapers. At that time, however, these jobs were not open to women. The only work Elizabeth could find was washing and ironing clothes in a laundry.

One day she read a story by a **newspaper editor** that made fun of women who were looking for jobs usually done only by men. Eighteen-year-old Elizabeth wrote to the paper telling how hard it was for a woman to find interesting work with good pay. The editor printed her letter and offered her a job as a reporter.

Right from the start, Elizabeth wanted to tell people about important problems. She would go anywhere to get a story. She knew that people might not talk to a reporter about these problems. To make sure she was getting the true story, Elizabeth would pretend to be someone else, not a reporter. For example, if she wanted to learn about the dangerous conditions in a factory, she would take a job there and then describe what she found.

When she was twenty-one, Elizabeth moved to New York. She hoped her experience in Pittsburgh would help her get a job at the *New York World*. This newspaper was well known for its reports on serious problems. But she soon learned that the New York newspapers were not hiring women reporters.

For months Elizabeth looked for work without success. When she was almost out of money, she decided to try just one more time at the *World*. She pushed herself into the editor's office and explained that she needed a job. The editor agreed to hire her if she could get herself admitted to a mental hospital as a patient. He wanted her to write about what it was like.

Elizabeth pretended she was mentally ill and stayed in the hospital for ten days. Her story telling about the hospital's awful conditions became front-page news. It brought about important changes in how the hospital cared for its patients.

After two years of writing about many kinds of problems in New York City, Elizabeth wanted something different. People were talking about a new book by the Frenchman Jules Verne. It was called *Around the World in Eighty Days.* Elizabeth decided she would try to beat the travel time set in the book. She convinced the *New York World* to pay for her trip. As she traveled, Elizabeth sent stories to the newspaper describing her adventures. Everywhere she went people were cheering her on. She made the trip in seventy-two days, six hours.

Elizabeth had become an admired, successful reporter. People enjoyed reading her stories. They knew a "Nellie Bly" story might talk about an important problem or it might be entertaining, but it would never be boring.

Elizabeth married in 1895 and stopped working as a reporter. But years later, after her husband's death, she returned to newspaper reporting. When Elizabeth died suddenly of **pneumonia** in 1922, she was still fighting to improve people's lives.

· · · HELPFUL VOCABULARY · · ·

investigative reporter: a person who thinks of a possible story, finds out what is true, and then writes about it

newspaper editor: a person who corrects and checks something written so that it is ready to be printed

pneumonia: a disease in which the lungs become inflamed and fill with thick fluid

THINKING ABOUT WHAT YOU HAVE READ

1. Where did Elizabeth Cochrane get her first newspaper job?

   _____

2. How did Elizabeth make sure her news stories were correct?

   _____

   _____

3. Why do you think Elizabeth liked her job?

   _____

   _____

4. Write the name of a well-known reporter.

   _____

   What do you know about this reporter?

   _____

   _____

5. Elizabeth wrote about many unfair things. If she were still living, what do you think she should write about?

   _____

   _____

6. How did newspaper editors help Elizabeth?

   _____

   _____

7. Elizabeth was trying to beat the travel time set in *Around the World in Eighty Days*. How much faster was she?

_____

8. If you could break a world record, which one would it be? Explain why.

_____

_____

_____

WORKING WITH WORDS

What new words did you learn from the story?

_____ _____ _____

Try to use two of them in sentences.

_____

_____

Some words sound alike but are spelled differently and have different meanings. These words are called **homophones.** For example, _meat_ and _meet_.

I like the _meat_ that was served at the restaurant.

Did you _meet_ your friend at the beach?

See if you can fill in the homophone pairs. Choose your answers from the following words.

beat   cent   new   red   would   beet   knew   read   sent   wood

To get her stories, Elizabeth _____ pretend to be some-one else.

Is maple a good _____ to burn in a fireplace?

Elizabeth _____ the newspaper editor's story.

These tomatoes are _____, but they are still not ripe.

People were talking about the _____ book *Around the World in Eighty Days.*

She _____ the answers to all the questions on the test.

Elizabeth tried to _____ the travel time set in *Around the World in Eighty Days.*

My aunt makes a wonderful _____ soup.

As she traveled, Elizabeth _____ stories to the *New York World* telling of her adventures.

Years ago some candies cost only one _____ each.

An **antonym** is a word that means the opposite of another word. *Up* is an antonym for *down.* Write an antonym for each of the following words.

first   _____   dangerous   _____

earlier   _____   awful   _____

interesting   _____   cheering   _____

How many adjectives (describing words) can you think of that tell what Elizabeth was like? Try to write at least three.

_____

_____

WRITING SKILLS

If Elizabeth were still alive, what would you like to ask her? Write three questions.

1. _____

2. _____

3. _____

Now write Elizabeth a letter and be sure to include your questions.

Dear _____,

_____

_____

_____

_____

_____

Sincerely,

_____

A **paragraph** is a group of sentences that talk about the same topic. Write a paragraph that tells about Elizabeth Cochrane's life. The topic sentence and the concluding sentence have been written for you. Write three other sentences that explain and support the topic sentence.

Elizabeth Cochrane led an exciting life.

_____

_____

_____

_____

She did things that many people just dream of doing.

What do you think that a doctor for a sports team does?

_____

_____

Dr. Susan Scott
1948–

Susan Scott loves her job working as the doctor of the Liberty, a professional basketball team for women. She says, "It is lots of fun because the players are great patients. When they are injured, they are very motivated to get well. They follow every instruction I give, and they are very willing to do as much **physical therapy** as needed."

Until recently, there were few professional women's sports teams of any kind in the United States. Many of the women

18

who wanted to play professional basketball had to find teams in Europe and Japan. Now they are very happy to be playing in their own country. They know that for women their jobs are **unique.** Susan says, "Their excitement is catching. I know that very few doctors are able to work with a basketball team, so I have a unique position, too. I treat everything from sore throats to **jammed** fingers and sprains."

If a player is injured during a game, Susan has to work quickly because the team must continue without the injured player. If the player is not badly hurt, Susan quickly fixes her up and sends her back into the game.

Susan was born in 1948 and grew up in New Milford, New Jersey. She says that as a child she had no special interest in science. But she does remember how much she loved seeing how things were put together. When Susan was thirteen, she took apart her uncle's old car and then put it back together. Even though she worked as a **volunteer** in a hospital as a teenager, she had no particular interest in medicine.

It was not until her third year of college that she decided to become a doctor. During her medical training, one of her teachers asked her to study hand surgery for a year. Susan now finds that year of study very useful as she works with her team. The players often get hand injuries from moving the ball around and from falling on the basketball court.

Susan feels rewarded when she helps the players. By working with the Liberty team, she has learned a lot about sports and women's role in sports. Susan enjoys watching the team play. She likes taking her two teenage children to the games because they also love the games and enjoy meeting the players. In her free time, Susan relaxes by biking and camping with her family.

··· HELPFUL VOCABULARY ···

physical therapy: the treatment of an injury by using massage, exercise, or heat rather than drugs

unique: being the only one of its kind

jammed: bruised or crushed

volunteer: a person who offers to help or does something by choice and without pay

THINKING ABOUT WHAT YOU HAVE READ

1. Where did Susan Scott grow up?

_____

2. How do we know that Susan liked to find out how things worked?

_____

_____

3. How are the Liberty players wonderful patients?

_____

_____

4. During a game, why does Susan have to work quickly?

_____

_____

5. Susan Scott has an unusual job. What are some other unusual jobs?

_____

_____

How could you find out about unusual jobs?

_____

_____

6. Susan says that her job has helped her learn about women's role in sports. What are some of the things you think Susan learned?

_____

_____

_____

_____

WORKING WITH WORDS

What new words did you learn from the story?

_____   _____   _____

Try to use two of them in sentences.

_____

_____

How are a fox, a dog, a bear, a cat, and a cow alike? If you said that they are all animals, you are right. Now read the following sets of words and explain how they are alike.

basketball   tennis   hockey   football   baseball

_____

Yankees   Rangers   Lakers   Knicks   Red Sox

_____

hoop   bat   puck   racket   roller blades

_____

doctor   teacher   plumber   cook   pilot

_____

Japan   Australia   Brazil   Canada   Spain

_____

Look at the following pair of words: *bicycle* and *water skis*. How are they alike and how are they different? We can say that both are used for fun, but one is used on land and the other on water.

Now look at these pairs of words. First write about how they are alike and then about how they are different.

doctor—dentist

_____

_____

basketball sneakers—jersey

_____

_____

cough medicine—Band-Aid

_____

_____

coach—player

_____

_____

A **synonym** is a word that has the same or almost the same meaning as another word. *Fix* is a synonym for *repair*.

Susan says that the players are **great** patients. What are two synonyms for **great**?

_____

The players are very **happy** to be playing in their own country. Write a synonym for **happy**.

_____

Sometimes players get **injured.** Write a synonym for **injured.**

_____

WRITING SKILLS

When Susan was a child, she loved taking things apart and putting them back together. Write and tell about something you like to do. Write at least three sentences.

_____

_____

_____

_____

What are three questions you would like to ask the Liberty players?

1. _____

2. _____

3. _____

Write a paragraph about your favorite athlete. First write a topic sentence that tells what you are writing about. Next write three sentences that tell about your topic. Then write a concluding sentence that brings your paragraph to a close.

_____

_____

_____

_____

_____

_____

Courtesy of the Collection of the New York Historical Society

José Martí
1853–1895

What was José Martí's greatest wish? He wanted his country, Cuba, a colony of Spain, to be free. Even though Spain had no plan to give independence to Cuba, **José** refused to give up his dream. His "Cuba Libre" or free-Cuba campaign resulted in the Cuban Revolution of 1895.

Even when José was a child growing up in Havana, he loved his country very much. One of his favorite teachers also wanted a better life for Cubans. He often talked with José about how badly the Spanish treated the Cuban people, how they **discriminated** against them, and how they made them pay unfair taxes.

In 1868 Cuba's first war for independence from Spain began. José was happy that he could secretly help with publishing newspapers that demanded a free Cuba. He also wrote a poem about people who would give their lives to make Cuba free.

Later that year the Spanish leaders found a letter José and a friend had written. It criticized another student for volunteering for the Spanish army. José was arrested and sentenced to six years of hard labor in a prison **quarry**. José's parents were able to get his sentence changed, and he was moved to a prison cell. But after a few months in prison, he was ordered to leave Cuba and was told to live in Spain.

After graduating from a university in Spain, José traveled to Mexico, where he got a job working as a **journalist**. But when a dictator came to power, José decided to leave the country. He wanted to live in a place where he could work and be free. From there he traveled to many different places, working as a writer in Guatemala and Venezuela.

Then in 1881 José moved to New York City. Luckily, he was such a talented writer that he could live from the money he earned writing articles for newspapers in North and South America. He also wrote beautiful poetry. Along with his writing, José spent a lot of his time working for Cuban independence. In 1892 he formed the Cuban Revolutionary Party. He traveled in the United States organizing patriotic clubs, especially in Florida among the Cuban tobacco workers. He was a powerful speaker. When he gave a speech, his audience listened with complete attention.

José asked Cubans to fight for an independent country. He said there should be justice and equality not only for Cubans but for all people, including Spaniards who decided to stay on the island.

José tried in many different ways to bring about the changes that Cubans needed, but nothing seemed to succeed. Finally, he wrote and signed a plan for an **uprising** in Cuba. On February 24, 1895, small groups of soldiers began to fight the Spaniards throughout Cuba. José said this was a "just and necessary war."

He had never been in battle, but he was eager to go to war for his country. He returned to Cuba. On May 19, 1895, in his first fight against enemy troops, José was killed at Dos Rios, Cuba. Today, however, he still lives as the father of Cuban independence.

· · · HELPFUL VOCABULARY · · ·

José: José Martí is known to most Latin Americans as Martí

discriminate: to treat some people differently from others for unfair reasons

quarry: a place where stone is cut or blasted out of the ground

journalist: a writer who works for a newspaper or magazine

uprising: a revolt against a government or other authority; a rebellion

THINKING ABOUT WHAT YOU HAVE READ

1. José lived in several countries. Write their names.

_____

_____

2. What was José Martí's greatest wish?

_____

3. How did the Spanish treat the Cubans?

_____

_____

4. When José was a teenager, how did he fight for independence?

_____

_____

5. How did José earn money?

_____

6. What do you know about Cuba?

_____

_____

_____

WORKING WITH WORDS

What new words did you learn from the story?

_____   _____   _____

Use two of them in sentences.

_____

_____

Some words sound alike but are spelled differently and have different meanings. These words are called **homophones.** For example, _heel_ and _heal_.

See if you can fill in the puzzle with the homophone pairs. First fill in the words going across. Then fill in the words going down.

Across

1. José Martí wanted Cubans **to** be free.

   I had _____ much to eat.

2. José grew up **in** Havana.

   My parents stayed at an old _____.

3. **Where** did José live?

   Did she _____ a new dress to the party?

4. José wrote, "Let us **be** free."

   A _____ sting is painful.

Down

5. The Cubans had to pay **high** taxes.

   Did you say "_____" to your neighbor?

6. Are those **new** shoes for school?

   He _____ all his lines for the class play.

7. The **main** character in José's poem is a patriot.

   The horse's _____ is thick.

In the story we learn that José said the Cuban war for independence was a "just and necessary war." What did he mean?

_____

_____

_____

WRITING SKILLS

Imagine that José Martí is going to give a speech. List three things he might talk about. Then make a poster to invite people to come.

_____

_____

_____

If you could ask José Martí three questions about his life, what would you ask?

1._____

2._____

3._____

Who are some other patriots you know? Write their names and a little about them.

_____

_____

_____

_____

_____

_____

_____

Why is fireproofing important?

_____

_____

Courtesy of Ms. Patricia Billings

Patricia Jean Billings
1926–

"The lady has stumbled onto something big," said a fire investigator after members of the Kansas City Fire Department performed a test on two sheds. One was made of normal materials and the other was made of Geobond. When both buildings were set on fire, the building made of ordinary materials went up in flames, but the one made of Geobond did not burn.

Who is the woman who invented Geobond, and how did she do it? Patricia Jean Billings was born in Clinton, Missouri.

She attended Kansas City Junior College and studied science and art but never got a college degree. Instead she worked for a short time as a **medical technician** and then quit her job when she got married.

Patricia returned to studying art in 1956 when she was living in Texas. She loved making **sculptures** of cowboys, horses, and birds from **plaster of paris.** Patricia sold her work to **local** shops and later opened one of her own in Kansas City where she sold her sculptures.

One day in the late 1960s, Patricia was carving the figure of a plaster swan; by accident she knocked it to the floor. The swan broke into hundreds of pieces. Patricia had worked four months on the piece and was very upset. She promised herself that she would make a material that was better than plaster of paris. She said she needed "something I could **cast** statues with that would give me details but wouldn't break."

First Patricia tried to strengthen the plaster of paris by adding a little bit of cement to it. But the mixture was **brittle** and could not be used for sculpting. A friend who was a scientist told her why she had failed. Plaster of paris, also known as gypsum ore, will melt in cement.

Later Patricia went on a trip to Italy and looked at famous paintings made on plaster, which had survived for hundreds of years. Then she went to the library and read magazines where she found that hundreds of years ago artists had strengthened plaster by using a cementlike material with a **catalyst.** The catalyst changed the chemical ingredients of the two materials so that they fastened together. Patricia tried to reinvent the recipe. She says that sometimes "instead of going ahead, you need to go back" to look for something.

After working eight years, Patricia thought she had the right mixture. She made a ten-inch statue and sent it to a scientist, who was impressed with how strong it was. Over the next eight years she perfected her product, which she called Geobond. She won't tell anyone the exact recipe, but says that it is made by mixing cement and gypsum with some ingredients you can buy easily in a store.

Patricia has formed a small company, Geobond International, in Kansas City. Geobond, in addition to being a good material for sculpture, is extremely fire-resistant. Geobond will not burn, even if it is heated to 6,500 degrees. Now it is being tested as a fireproof coating for airplanes. Patricia had started out looking for something to use for making sculptures, but she discovered that the material she invented had another more important use.

This seventy-three-year-old grandmother says that in a few years she may sell her part of the company. She would like to have more time for her artwork and for travel.

··· HELPFUL VOCABULARY ···

medical technician: a person who analyzes blood and other materials for a doctor

sculpture: a piece of art, made by carving or molding stone, clay, or other materials into a design or figure

plaster of paris: a material that is mixed with water to make a thick, pasty, quick-setting mixture for creating casts and statues

local: having to do with a particular place

cast: to shape by pouring a soft material into a mold to harden

brittle: very easily broken

catalyst: something that causes or speeds up change or action

THINKING ABOUT WHAT YOU HAVE READ

1. What did Patricia study in college?

   _____

2. What kind of sculptures did Patricia make?

   _____

   _____

3. Why was the plaster swan Patricia made in the late 1960s so important?

   _____

   _____

4. What is special about Geobond?

   _____

   _____

5. Who would find Geobond very useful?

   _____

   _____

6. According to the story, how long did Patricia work to develop Geobond?

   _____

   _____

WORKING WITH WORDS

Patricia Billings says that sometimes "instead of going ahead, you need to go back" to look for something. What does she mean?

_____

_____

List as many adjectives (describing words) as you can that might tell what Patricia Billings is like. Try to think of at least four.

_____

_____

A **synonym** is a word that has the same or almost the same meaning as another word. _Fast_ is a synonym for _quick._ Think of a synonym for these words from the story.

survived for hundreds of years

_____ for hundreds of years

attended college

_____ college

returned to studying

_____ studying

loved making sculptures

_____ making sculptures

opened a shop

_____ a shop

famous paintings

_____ paintings

the **right** mixture

the _____ mixture

has **formed** a company

has _____ a company

WRITING SKILLS

How is Patricia's life an example of the proverb "If at first you don't succeed, try, try again"?

_____

_____

Imagine you are a news reporter who is watching the two sheds in the experiment with Geobond. Write about what you see and hear. Then draw a picture of the scene.

_____

_____

_____

_____

What does a surgeon do?

_____

_____

Courtesy of Moorland-Springarn Research Center, Howard University, Washington, D.C.

Dr. Daniel Hale Williams
1856–1931

In 1893 the headline of a Chicago newspaper shouted, "SEWED UP HIS HEART!" Dr. Daniel Hale Williams had performed the first successful **surgery** on the heart. After fifty-one days in the hospital, the patient left fully recovered. "Dr. Dan," as he was called by his patients, was suddenly famous.

Dan was born in Hollidaysburg, Pennsylvania, in 1856. When he was eleven, his father died. Dan's mother arranged for him to be **apprenticed** to a shoemaker in Baltimore, Maryland. Then she moved with her daughters to Illinois.

But Dan did not want to be a shoemaker, so after a year he left the job. He traveled west to visit his mother and sisters, then went north to Wisconsin. He learned how to be a barber. He settled in Janesville and started to work for an African-American barber named Harry Anderson. Dan lived with the Andersons, who treated him like a member of their family.

In 1877 Dan graduated from high school. He became interested in medicine and began working as an apprentice for the town's doctor. In exchange for helping the doctor, he learned about medicine. After a few years, the doctor advised Dan to complete his training by studying at the Chicago Medical College. To pay for the school, Dan used the little money he had saved and borrowed the rest from Harry Anderson. After he graduated in 1883, Dan set up his own office and became a well-liked and successful surgeon.

At that time many hospitals refused to treat African-American patients, and the few that did often put these patients in the dirtiest areas. Very few African Americans were admitted to medical schools. Those who became doctors were not allowed to operate in most hospitals, and no nursing school would admit an African-American student. Dan wanted to change this. All people should have good medical care, he believed, and African-American doctors and nurses should also be able to have fine training.

Dan said, "There must be a hospital for Negroes, but not a **Negro** hospital." He decided to start a new kind of hospital—one to be owned, **staffed,** and managed by African Americans and whites together. It would be open to doctors and patients of all races and would be the first hospital to train African-American nurses. With the help and support of many people, Dan opened the Provident Hospital and Training School in Chicago in 1891.

Three years later, President Grover Cleveland appointed Dan chief surgeon of Freedman's Hospital, a very large hospital in Washington, D.C. Freedman's was connected to Howard University, an African-American college with a medical school. Dan improved the running of the hospital by dividing the work into different departments. He started a second nurses' training school there. In addition, he provided many opportunities for the medical students and nurses to observe and help with the care of the patients.

In Washington, Dan met Alice Johnson, a school teacher, whom he married in 1898. They moved to Chicago where Dan continued to perform **groundbreaking** surgery. He often wrote down what he did in his operations so that other doctors could learn from his work.

In 1920 Dan and his wife retired to their summer home in northern Michigan. The Provident Hospital, which Dan started, is no longer in operation, but it served as a model for forty new hospitals in twenty different states.

· · · HELPFUL VOCABULARY · · ·

surgery: an operation

apprentice: a person who works for a skilled worker in order to learn a trade or art

Negro: an African American; in recent times the term *African American* has replaced the word *Negro*

staffed: provided with workers

groundbreaking: being the first to do or try a particular activity

THINKING ABOUT WHAT YOU HAVE READ

1. Where was Dan born?

_____

_____

2. Why did Daniel Williams become famous?

_____

_____

3. Besides being a doctor, what other jobs was Dan trained to do?

_____

_____

4. How did the Andersons help Dan?

_____

_____

5. How did Dr. Daniel Williams help African Americans?

_____

_____

_____

6. How was Provident Hospital the first of its kind?

_____

_____

_____

7. In addition to heart surgery, what do you think are some other difficult operations?

_____

_____

_____

WORKING WITH WORDS

In the story we learn that Dan performed **groundbreaking** surgery. Use **groundbreaking** in a sentence.

_____

_____

You can "paint" a picture using paint or words. Look at the picture of Dr. Daniel Hale Williams and think about the story. Use words to "paint" a picture of what he was like.

_____   _____   _____

_____

Now use words to "paint" a picture of what you are like.

_____   _____   _____

_____

Look at the descriptions of some of the tools a doctor uses. Now write the name that goes with the description. The first one has been done for you.

Stethoscope an instrument used by doctors to listen to heartbeats and other sounds in the body

_____ a device used to find out how heavy something is

_____ an instrument used to measure temperature

_____ a strip of cloth or other material used to cover or wrap a cut or other wound

_____ a stiff form that is shaped around a part of the body to hold a broken bone in place so that it can heal

When you visit a hospital, you see many things. Try to list six things you would see.

_____   _____   _____

_____   _____   _____

WRITING SKILLS

A storyboard is a set of pictures that tell a story. It is often used to plan a movie. Make a storyboard telling about Dr. Dan's life. In each box draw a picture. Show the different things Dr. Dan did.

```
1


```

```
2


```

```
3


```

```
4


```

```
5


```

Write what is happening in each box.

1. Dan worked for a shoemaker.

2. _____

3. _____

4. _____

5. _____

Why do you think people run long-distance races?

_____

_____

CORBIS—UPI ©

Kathrine Switzer
1947–

Today it seems surprising, but not that long ago women were told they couldn't and shouldn't run. They were not allowed to **compete** in **marathons.** Then in 1967 twenty-year-old Kathrine Switzer surprised the world by completing the twenty-six-mile, 385-yard Boston Marathon.

Kathrine, who was born in 1947, grew up in Vienna, Virginia. She says that her parents always encouraged her. When Kathrine was a freshman in high school, she was afraid she would not make the field hockey team. So her father told her to get in shape by running a mile each day.

When people saw her running, they thought she was crazy. But Kathrine discovered that she loved running and that it gave her lots of energy and confidence. Kathrine made the field hockey team; later she trained for the basketball and **lacrosse** teams by running a mile each day. The three sports, however, were not enough of a workout, so she began to run two or three miles a day. When Kathrine saw women running in the Olympics on television, she decided to quit her other sports and "be a runner."

After high school, she went to Lynchburg College in Virginia. When eleven members of the male track team were dropped because of poor grades, the track coach asked her if she could run a mile. A big meet was coming, and he needed more people to help the team. Kathrine ran, but finished last in her race. Some people thought it was great that she competed, but others said nasty things to her or laughed as she walked by.

A year later, Kathrine **transferred** to Syracuse University in New York State. At that time, Syracuse had no women's teams playing against other colleges, so Kathrine trained with the men's track team. She surprised her coach, Arnie Briggs, when she ran twenty-six miles and more in practice. She convinced Arnie to take her to the Boston Marathon. This famous race had begun over seventy years earlier. Many people thought it was too difficult for women to run, even though a woman had run most of the distance one year.

Arnie insisted that Kathrine apply for the race as all the men runners had to do. Since she always signed her work at school with her initials, she signed the application form in the same way, K.V. Switzer. The people directing the marathon did not realize that K.V. Switzer was a woman.

On the day of the race, just a few miles after Kathrine began running, a furious official screamed at her to give him her number and to get out of the race. He grabbed her. Arnie told the official to leave her alone. There was a fight and someone shoved the official off the course.

Kathrine was scared and angry. She says that for a few seconds she thought she would quit, but she realized, "If I quit now, people will say women can't do it." By the time Kathrine finished the race, she had decided two things—she was going to become a better athlete, and she was going to create more opportunities in sports for women.

In the years that followed, Kathrine ran in many marathons and won the 1974 New York City Marathon. She worked as a sportswriter and an award-winning television sports broadcaster. Kathrine has "made things happen in sports for women." She wanted a women's marathon included in the Olympics. She thought of a plan; there would be a series of distance races for women with the last race an international marathon.

In 1977 Avon Cosmetics Company agreed to sponsor her plan and hired her to direct the program. Within five years, there were long-distance races in twenty-one countries. Kathrine says that she will never forget how eager women were to compete. In Brazil and Thailand women were "turning up with no shoes, no shoes at all." These races helped convince the International Olympic Committee to include the women's marathon event as part of the Olympics. The first was run in 1984.

Kathrine believes that running gives people strong minds as well as strong bodies. She says that running is still the most important part of her day.

· · · HELPFUL VOCABULARY · · ·

marathon: a long race that tests endurance

lacrosse: a game played by two teams in which the players use sticks with a net on one end to throw, catch, and carry a ball to the goal

compete: to try to win or gain something from another or others

transfer: to move from one person or place to another

THINKING ABOUT WHAT YOU HAVE READ

1. How long is the Boston Marathon?

   _____

2. Why did Kathrine like running?

   _____

   _____

3. Why didn't the Boston Marathon officials know Kathrine was a woman?

   _____

   _____

4. What did Kathrine learn from the Boston Marathon?

   _____

   _____

5. How did Kathrine feel when the official grabbed her? What did she do?

   _____

   _____

6. Why do you think Kathrine's plan for a series of long-distance races was important?

   _____

   _____

7. How do you think women felt when they ran in a marathon
   for the first time?

   _____

   _____

WORKING WITH WORDS

An **antonym** is a word that means the opposite of another word. *Big* is an antonym for *little*. Write an antonym for each of the following words.

hard _____   found _____

late _____   finish _____

furious _____   always _____

strong _____   quit _____

A **definition** explains the meaning of a word or group of words. A definition of the word *house* is "a building in which people live." Try to write a good definition of the following words.

workout

_____

nasty

_____

convince

_____

international

_____

hire

_____

Sometimes words have more than one meaning. In the following sentences, the word in bold print has one meaning. Write what it is on the first line. Then on the second line, write a sentence in which the word in bold print has a different meaning.

Example: Jack likes his steak **rare.** *Rare* means cooked only slightly. Rubies are *rare* jewels.

Bill and Jane have a lemonade **stand.**

_____

_____

In the summer it gets **light** early.

_____

_____

Eleven members of the track team had **poor** grades.

_____

_____

It is **hard** to believe that women didn't always run in races.

_____

_____

José threw a **pass** to Mike.

_____

_____

WRITING SKILLS

Kathrine says that her parents always encouraged her. How do your parents encourage you?

_____

_____

_____

_____

During the marathon, a race official told Kathrine she should stop, but she didn't. Was Kathrine right to disobey the official? Explain your answer.

_____

_____

_____

_____

_____

What is something you enjoy doing for hours?

_____

_____

Al Hirschfeld
1903–2003

For over seventy years, people enjoyed looking at Al Hirschfeld's drawings of theater and movie stars in the *New York Times.* With just a few lines from his drawing pen, he is able to show what our greatest entertainers are like.

Al Hirschfeld was born in St. Louis, Missouri, and by the time he was eight he was painting and even sculpting. A young painter told Hirschfeld's parents that they should move to New York so that their son could study art. Because his mother believed that Hirschfeld was very talented, she convinced his father to move.

In New York, Hirschfeld went to a boys' school that taught printmaking. At night he went to art school. When he was fourteen, his mother took him to a Broadway musical. He loved it, and afterwards he went as often as he could.

Al Hirschfeld said that his career began by accident in 1926. One day he went to the theater with Dick Maney. He was a **press agent** for the play they were seeing. Hirschfeld was not interested in the play, and during the performance he began scribbling on the program. When Dick Maney saw what his friend had done, he suggested that Hirschfeld do a drawing on a clean piece of paper. Dick Maney offered to take the drawing around to the newspapers to see if he could get one of them to print it. The following Sunday the picture was on the front theater page of a leading newspaper. Hirschfeld said that he was **flabbergasted.** From that time, he did drawings for many New York City newspapers. A year later, when the *New York Times* asked him to draw only for them, he agreed.

Hirschfeld worked seven days a week. But he said, "It isn't work, kid. It's luxury. Pure luxury. I don't call it work." Sitting in a barber's chair, which he had for more than fifty years, Hirschfeld would lean over an old drawing board for hours at a time. First, he made a pencil drawing. Using ink, he outlined the major features and **characteristics** of the subject. Then he erased the original pencil drawing. A drawing could be ready in a couple of hours or sometimes it could take three days.

Whenever he went to the **preview** of a show, Hirschfeld brought an eight-by-ten-inch sketchbook with a supply of pencils taped inside its cover. Sketching in the dark, he filled in about half the pad with quickly jotted drawings. He wrote surprising notes to himself such as "fried eggs for eyes" along with short descriptions of the character, costume, and scenery. When he got home, he looked at his sketches and his notes. Then recalling what he saw, he made a drawing. His pictures were very **focused** so that the viewer could get the idea of the show. Sometimes Hirschfeld put sixty people into one drawing!

When his daughter Nina was born, he started writing her name in his pictures. Shortly after he started doing this, he got a letter suggesting that there should be some way to tell how many *Ninas* are written in each drawing. So Hirschfeld put a number in each drawing which tells how many *Ninas* there are. A lot of fans enjoy hunting for them.

Al Hirschfeld made from ten to twelve thousand drawings. Almost every museum in the country has a Hirschfeld drawing. Even the United States Postal Service has issued a series of stamps using his work. When asked which was his favorite drawing, Hirschfeld said, "The one I'm working on. If it works out, that will be my favorite."

· · · HELPFUL VOCABULARY · · ·

sculpting: making or carving figures in stone, clay, metal, or any other material

press agent: a person who lets people know that a particular event is going to happen

flabbergasted: astonished

characteristic: a quality or feature that belongs to and helps to identify a person or thing

preview: a showing of something ahead of time

focus: to fix or direct the attention

THINKING ABOUT WHAT YOU HAVE READ

1. What does Al Hirschfeld do for a living?

_____

2. Where did he study art?

_____

_____

3. How did he become interested in the theater?

_____

4. How was Dick Maney important to Hirschfeld's career?

_____

_____

5. What newspaper prints Al Hirschfeld's drawings?

_____

6. What word does Hirschfeld put in his drawings? Why?

_____

_____

7. What is surprising about Al Hirschfeld's life?

_____

_____

WORKING WITH WORDS

How are a drawing and a painting the same?

_____

How are they different?

_____

_____

List the tools mentioned in the story that Al Hirschfeld uses.
Then add other tools that an artist might use.

_____

_____

How are a ring, a necklace, and a bracelet alike? If you said
that they are all pieces of jewelry, you are right. Now read the
following sets of words and explain how they are alike.

stage   lights   seats   curtain   scenery

_____

print   oil painting   sketch   watercolor   drawing

_____

crayons   oils   pencils   paints   markers

_____

play   concert   magic show   ballet   musical

_____

actor   stagehands   usher   ticket taker   actress

_____

WRITING SKILLS

If you were interviewing Al Hirschfeld for a television program, what are three questions you would like to ask him?

1. _____

2. _____

3. _____

Hirschfeld thinks his work is "pure luxury." What do you think he means?

_____

_____

_____

What do you do that is "pure luxury"?

_____

_____

_____

A storyboard is a set of pictures that tell a story. It is often used to plan a movie. Make a storyboard telling about Al Hirschfeld's life. In each box draw a picture. Show the different things Al did.

1	2

3	4

5

Write what is happening in each box.

1. _____

2. _____

3. _____

4. _____

5. _____

What hair products do you like to use?

_____

_____

Courtesy of Moorland-Springarn Research Center, Howard University, Washington, D.C.

Sarah Breedlove Walker
1867–1919

The first African-American woman to become famous for running her own company was Sarah Breedlove Walker. She was born on a Louisiana cotton **plantation** in 1867. By the time she was seven, both her parents had died. In order to make enough money to stay alive, she and her sister began working as **laundresses.** A few years later Sarah moved to Vicksburg, Mississippi, where she married. When she was seventeen, her daughter Lelia was born. Then just two years later, her husband died in an accident.

In 1888 Sarah moved with Lelia to St. Louis, Missouri, where she had heard there were higher paying jobs for laundresses. One day as Sarah was bending over her washboard scrubbing clothes, she thought, "What are you going to do when you grow old, and your back gets stiff?" But she could not think of a way she could better her life.

Once, when she saw a beautifully dressed African-American woman, Sarah thought, "If I improve the way I look, maybe I will be more self-confident." Sarah's hair was broken and showed her scalp in several places. She tried different hair lotions to keep her hair from falling out. Then Sarah started making some **products** of her own and using them. Soon she found that her hair was growing in.

Sarah decided to move to Denver where some relatives lived. For a time she worked as a cook for a druggist, while she continued to develop her hair products. Sarah asked the druggist about the **ingredients** for the hair preparations she was making. She came up with three products, which she made at home—a hair grower, a **pomade,** and a shampoo. Early in 1906, Sarah married Charles Walker. He was a newspaper salesperson, and he became her business partner.

During the next few years, Sarah developed her business. She knocked on people's doors, giving free demonstrations and selling her products. Women were impressed by her self-confidence. Hoping to look like her, they bought Sarah's products. Within a few months she was making thirty-five dollars a week. This was more than twenty times the salary of the average African-American woman worker. Soon Sarah started showing other women how to sell her products. She called these women Walker agents. She also developed a big mail-order business.

In 1908 Sarah moved to Pittsburgh and opened a beauty parlor and a training school for Walker saleswomen. Two years later she moved to Indianapolis and opened a factory. Soon Sarah's company had 1,600 Walker agents. These women made as much money in one week as they would make in a month at any other job open to African-American women. By 1916 there were 20,000 Walker agents in the United States, Central America, and the Caribbean.

Sarah was the first African-American woman to become a **self-made** millionaire. Besides giving large amounts of money to help African Americans, Sarah traveled across the country encouraging African-American women. She said, "Don't sit down and wait for the opportunities to come. Get up and make them!"

· · · HELPFUL VOCABULARY · · ·

plantation: a large estate or farm worked by the laborers who live there

laundress: a woman employed to do washing or washing and ironing

product: anything that is made

ingredient: any one of the parts that go into a mixture

pomade: a dressing for the hair that has a pleasing smell

self-made: made by oneself

THINKING ABOUT WHAT YOU HAVE READ

1. Where was Sarah Breedlove Walker born?

    _____

2. After her parents died, how did Sarah support herself?

    _____

3. At first, how did Sarah sell her hair products?

    _____

4. What was a Walker agent?

    _____

    _____

5. Why would a woman want to become a Walker agent?

    _____

    _____

6. In 1910 what kinds of jobs do you think a woman could
    have in Sarah's company?

    _____

    _____

WORKING WITH WORDS

Sarah invented several different hair products. List as many things as you can that people use to take care of their hair.

_____   _____   _____

_____   _____   _____

List five things you find at a beauty salon or a barbershop.

_____   _____   _____

_____   _____   _____

How many adjectives (describing words) can you think of that tell what Sarah was like. Try to write at least four.

_____

_____

Sarah started a mail-order business. Explain what this is.

_____

_____

Write the name of a mail-order business you know.

_____

WRITING SKILLS

Pretend you are writing a story for a magazine about Sarah Breedlove Walker's life. List three important events in Sarah's life.

1._____

2._____

3._____

Now write your story. Begin your story with a topic sentence that tells what you are writing about. Include the three important events you listed above. Be sure to write a concluding sentence.

_____

_____

_____

_____

_____

_____

African-American women were delighted when they could get a job as a Walker agent. Some of these women wrote to Sarah, telling her how the job had changed their lives. Pretend you are a Walker agent and write a letter to Sarah Breedlove Walker. Describe some of the people you sold hair products to and tell how the hair products helped them.

Dear Ms. Walker,

_____

_____

_____

_____

_____

_____

                                      Sincerely,

                                     _____

What is something you have dreamed of that seemed
impossible to get?

_____

_____

Photo by Tom Boulting

Sam Wanamaker
1919–1993

Sam Wanamaker had a dream. He wanted to rebuild
William Shakespeare's famous Globe Theater in London.
William Shakespeare, one of the world's greatest **playwrights,**
lived from 1564 to 1616. For more than twenty years, Sam
worked to make his dream come true.

When he was fourteen, Sam first learned about the Globe
Theater. He saw a large model of it at the Chicago World's Fair
and never forgot it. A few years later, Sam went off to college

in Iowa. A teacher offered him a part in a school play, and Sam discovered that he loved acting. After studying at a theater school in Chicago, he joined an acting company in Cleveland. This group was performing Shakespeare's plays in a theater that was a small copy of the Globe. It was around this time that Sam began to think of rebuilding the Globe Theater.

In 1949 Sam made his first visit to England. By that time he had become a well-known actor and director and was starring in a movie there. On his first day off, he went to look for the spot where the original Globe Theater had been. All he found was a small, blackened bronze **plaque** on a **brewery** wall. The plaque read, "Here stood Shakespeare's Globe." Sam wondered, "How could this be the only reminder of Shakespeare's theater?" He wanted to mark the spot in a better way.

Sam and his family moved to England. During the next years, he was very busy with work. Even so he never forgot his dream of recreating the Globe Theater. One day when his brother was visiting from Chicago, they took a walk to the place Sam had visited before. He showed his brother the blackened plaque and told him his idea of rebuilding the Globe. Suddenly his brother said, "If you're that **keen,** why don't you do something about it?" When they got home from their walk, Sam told his wife, "I'm going to do it myself."

Many people were against rebuilding the theater. They did not think that it was necessary to build another theater devoted to Shakespeare. They argued that it would cost too much money. They said it was not a good spot to build a theater because the area was run-down. They believed the people living there would not come to a play by Shakespeare.

But Sam did not give up his dream of wanting to introduce Shakespeare's plays to people who had not seen them. He wanted everyone to share his love of Shakespeare's works.

Doing everything he could, Sam raised the money for the theater. Using wood, **thatch,** and plaster, craftsmen constructed a building modeled as closely as possible on the first one. It stands near the location of the original Globe Theater.

In 1992, with the building only half-finished, Sam saw the first production of a play. Sadly, he never saw one of Shakespeare's plays performed at the Globe. He had been suffering from cancer for several years and died before it was completed. Today, during the summer months, many of Shakespeare's plays are performed in this theater.

When tour guides show visitors around the building, they say, "WS and SW—two very important initials, WS for William Shakespeare, the great playwright, and SW for Sam Wanamaker, the man who rebuilt his theater."

· · · HELPFUL VOCABULARY · · ·

playwright: a person who writes plays

plaque: a flat piece of wood or metal that is decorated and hung on a wall

brewery: a place where beer is made

keen: eager, full of enthusiasm

thatch: straw, reeds, or similar material that is used to cover a roof

THINKING ABOUT WHAT YOU HAVE READ

1. Who was William Shakespeare?

   _____

2. What was Sam Wanamaker's dream?

   _____

   _____

3. Why do you think Sam wanted to rebuild the Globe?

   _____

4. Why were some people against this idea?

   _____

   _____

5. How do you think Shakespeare's theater might have been different from our theaters today?

   _____

   _____

6. Sam had his dream for a long time. What made him start working on it?

   _____

   _____

   _____

WORKING WITH WORDS

What new vocabulary words did you learn from the story?

_____   _____   _____

Use two of them in sentences.

_____

_____

A **definition** explains the meaning of a word or group of words. A definition of the word _dove_ is "a small bird that looks like a pigeon." Write a definition for the words in bold print.

Sam Wanamaker had a **dream.**

_____

He saw a large **model** of the old Globe.

_____

He was **starring** in a movie there.

_____

Craftsmen **constructed** the theater.

_____

The area was **run-down.**

_____

He went to look for the spot where the **original** Globe Theater had been.

_____

Was the work **completed** before Sam died?

_____

Read the story again. Then fill in the bubbles in the picture with words that Sam and his brother might have said to each other on their walk.

WRITING SKILLS

Sam worked for many years so that his dream would come true. Write about something you have worked hard for. Write at least five sentences. Remember to write a topic and a concluding sentence.

_____

_____

_____

_____

_____

Sam had a dream. Write about a dream you have.

_____

_____

_____

_____

Pretend you are William Shakespeare writing a letter to Sam Wanamaker. What would you say?

Dear Sam,

_____

_____

_____

_____

_____

_____

Sincerely,

_____

_____

_____

Courtesy of Library of Congress, LC-USZ62-13459

Dr. Sara Josephine Baker
1873–1945

Now both men and women are doctors, but in 1891 when seventeen-year-old Sara Josephine Baker said that she wanted to be a doctor, everyone around her tried to talk her out of it.

Sara was born in 1873 into a well-to-do family in Poughkeepsie, New York. When she was sixteen, her comfortable and happy life changed forever. Her father and brother suddenly became sick from the drinking water and died. With only a small savings left for the family, Sara knew that she would have to work to support her mother and sister. She decided to become a doctor. In 1898 she graduated from the Women's Medical College in New York City, ranking second out of eighteen students.

Sara opened an office in New York City. Many people, however, did not want to go to a woman doctor. In her first year of practice Sara made only $185. Then in 1901 she got a job working as a **medical inspector** for New York City's department of health. There she was paid twice as much money as she had earned before.

Many poor people were dying from **contagious** diseases. Sara was assigned to work in one of these neighborhoods. She went alone to each **tenement,** checking for these diseases. What she saw made Sara want to help.

As many as 1,500 infants a week were dying in the poorest areas of the city. Sara realized that many of these babies died because people did not know how to stay healthy. She thought that the way to keep people from dying from disease was to keep them from falling ill. "Healthy people didn't die." This was a totally new idea. Sara went to people's homes teaching young mothers the basics of health care for their infants.

Her work was so good that she was promoted to a high position in the health department. Then in 1908 the city set up the world's first children's health department and asked Sara to be its head. Although the work would be difficult, she knew other doctors would be helping her. Sara would supervise an all-male staff. But when the men learned that a woman would be their boss, they all quit. She convinced each man to work for a month. Then if they still wanted to quit, she told them they could. At the end of the month, however, all were eager to continue the interesting and **challenging** work they had.

Sara developed many new programs to help save children's lives and improve their health. She saw that poor mothers often had milk that was not **pasteurized.** This caused it to spoil easily and led to illness. She set up "milk stations" where free or low-cost pasteurized milk was given out. She also started the "Little Mother's League" to teach baby care to children who were left in charge of their younger brothers and sisters.

When she learned that some infant clothes were so tight that they had **strangled** babies, she invented new, practical baby clothes. These opened down the front. A life insurance company handed out 200,000 of her clothing patterns.

Because of Sara's programs, infant deaths in the poorest areas of the city dropped from 1,500 a week to 300. Within fifteen years, New York had the lowest infant death rate in the world. When people in other countries learned about the success of Sara's programs, they were eager to use them, too.

Sara wanted children's health to become a major concern throughout the United States. She made a deal with herself. When all forty-eight states had started programs like hers, she would then retire to her farm in New Jersey. Later, Sara wrote of her work, "I can still see the light in a mother's eye when her baby was assured of health."

··· HELPFUL VOCABULARY ···

medical inspector: a doctor who checks for diseases that spread from person to person

contagious: able to spread from person to person

tenement: an old apartment building, usually in poor condition

challenging: making someone think, work, or try hard

pasteurized: heated to a specific temperature for a given period of time to kill germs that may be living in the milk

strangled: choked

THINKING ABOUT WHAT YOU HAVE READ

1. Why do you think people tried to convince Sara not to become a doctor?

   _____

2. When she was sixteen, how did Sara's life change?

   _____

   _____

3. Why do you think many people did not want to go to women doctors?

   _____

4. In the late 1800s many people doubted that women could be good doctors. Describe two events in Sara's life that are examples of this prejudice.

   _____

   _____

   _____

5. How did Sara help children stay healthy?

   _____

   _____

6. Look at the photo of Sara Josephine Baker in her office. How do you think your doctor's office is different from Sara's office?

   _____

   _____

WORKING WITH WORDS

Sara said that the way to keep people from dying from disease was to keep them from falling ill. "Healthy people didn't die." Explain what Sara meant.

_____

_____

Sometimes words have more than one meaning. Look at the following pairs of sentences. In the first sentence of each pair, look at how the word in bold print is used. Try to write what it means. Then write an answer to the question that follows it.

Sara had to work to **support** her mother and sister.

_____

What else can **support** mean?

_____

In her first year of **practice** Sara made only $185.

_____

What else can **practice** mean?

_____

Sara went **checking** for these diseases.

_____

What else can **checking** mean?

_____

Sara could see the **light** in a mother's eye.

_____

What else can **light** mean?

_____

An **antonym** is a word that means the opposite of another word. *Slow* is an antonym of *fast*. Write an antonym for these words.

father _____   poor _____

brother _____   first _____

many _____   everyone _____

work _____   live _____

A **synonym** is a word that has the same or almost the same meaning as another word. *Stop* is a synonym for *halt*. Write synonyms for the words in bold print.

She **wanted** to be a doctor. _____

Sara **made** only $185. _____

Free milk was **handed** out. _____

She also **started** the "Little Mother's League." _____

Her work was so **good** that she was promoted. _____

The idea was to keep people from falling **ill.** _____

WRITING SKILLS

Write a paragraph about Sara's life. Below is the topic sentence. Now write three supporting sentences. Then try to write a concluding sentence that explains what the paragraph has talked about.

    Sara Josephine Baker was an outstanding doctor.

_____

_____

_____

_____

_____

Make an ad for Sara's new baby clothes. On the lines below, list two reasons why people should buy these clothes. Then draw your advertisement in the box on the next page. Be sure to include the information you want people to learn.

_____

_____

_____

_____

Photo by Cheung Ching Ming

Maya Lin
1959–

Every year, two and a half million people file past the Vietnam Veterans Memorial in Washington, D.C. But how many of these people have heard of Maya Lin, the architectural student who designed it?

Maya was born and grew up in Athens, Ohio. Her parents had **emigrated** from China and taught at Ohio University. Her mother was a professor of English and Asian literature, and her father was an artist and dean of fine arts.

As a child Maya spent most of her free time alone, hiking in the woods, bird-watching, reading, and making pottery in her father's studio. While she was in high school, in addition to working part-time at McDonald's, Maya liked to try different crafts—silversmithing, rug weaving, candle making, "anything I could get my hands on."

In 1980 when Maya was a senior at Yale University, one of her professors asked the students in his class to enter a **competition** to design the Vietnam Veterans Memorial. Her simple but **bold** design called for two long, low, highly polished, black **granite** walls, coming together to form a shallow "V." The names of the nearly 58,000 dead and missing **veterans** of the Vietnam War would be written on the walls.

Out of 1,420 entries, Maya's design was chosen the winner. After the judges announced their decision, some people were very upset. They did not like her design and did not want it made. They believed it did not honor the people who died in the war. But Maya's design was built, and "the Wall" has given comfort to thousands of visitors who come each year to touch the names on its surface.

After receiving a master's degree in architecture from Yale, Maya moved to New York City. Now she tries to balance her love of both sculpture and architecture by doing many different kinds of projects. One outdoor sculpture she created was a series of low, grass-covered hills. In other sculptures she has used unusual materials such as lead, beeswax, and broken glass. Maya also has designed homes and a museum.

After the Vietnam Memorial, Maya's best known work is the Civil Rights Memorial in Montgomery, Alabama. This honors those killed in the fight for racial justice in the South. Her design was inspired by a quote from a speech by Martin Luther King Jr. This appears as part of the memorial: "We will not be satisfied until justice rolls down like water." Her design is a wall of water next to a round granite "water table," which lists the major events in the civil rights movement.

Maya said she "was surprised and moved when people started to cry" at the opening of the memorial in Montgomery. But in this work and many others, Maya has created pieces that invite people to touch them. When they do, they often feel powerful emotions.

Maya plans to continue working as both an architect and a sculptor: "Just doing one wouldn't be the full picture for me."

· · · HELPFUL VOCABULARY · · ·

emigrate: to leave one's country to live in another

competition: a contest

bold: standing out clearly

granite: a kind of rock that is very hard

veteran: a person who has served in the armed forces

THINKING ABOUT WHAT YOU HAVE READ

1. How did Maya Lin spend her high school years?

   _____

   _____

2. When Maya was studying architecture, why did her name appear in many newspapers?

   _____

3. What was Maya's design for the Vietnam Veterans Memorial like?

   _____

   _____

4. Why do you think people are comforted when they visit "the Wall"?

   _____

   _____

5. How was Maya Lin's design for the Civil Rights Memorial inspired by the words of Martin Luther King Jr.?

   _____

6. What are two examples of how Maya has allowed people to touch her memorials?

   _____

   _____

WORKING WITH WORDS

Explain what Maya Lin means when she says, "Just doing one wouldn't be the full picture for me."

_____

_____

Sometimes words have more than one meaning. *Moved* can mean "stirred a person's feelings" or "changed the place or direction of something."

Write down two meanings for the following words.

rolls

_____

_____

free

_____

_____

enter

_____

_____

shape

_____

_____

A **synonym** is a word that has the same or almost the same meaning as another word. *Kind* is a synonym for *nice.*

An **antonym** is a word that means the opposite of another word. *Hot* is an antonym for *cold.*

Write one synonym and one antonym for each of the following words.

	Synonym	**Antonym**
like	_____	_____
simple	_____	_____
powerful	_____	_____
sick	_____	_____
polished	_____	_____
push	_____	_____

WRITING SKILLS

Maya Lin leads an interesting life. List three things she has done that you would like to know more about.

1._____

2._____

3._____

Write a paragraph about Maya and include the things you have listed. Try to write both a topic and a concluding sentence.

_____

_____

_____

_____

_____

_____

_____

Imagine that you visited the Vietnam Veterans Memorial in Washington, D.C. Write a postcard to a friend, describing your visit to the memorial.

Dear _____,

_____

_____

_____

_____

Love,

_____

What is your favorite musical instrument and why?

_____

_____

Photo by Christian Steiner

Jaime Laredo
1941–

Jaime Laredo's life is filled with many different musical experiences. Besides being a violin soloist and a conductor, Jaime plays the violin and the **viola** with a group.

Jaime was born in Cochabamba, Bolivia. When he was five years old, his parents took him to hear a **string quartet,** and this experience changed his life. "I told my father right there that I wanted to play the violin. I loved the sound. It sounded to me like a beautiful human voice." A teacher noticed Jaime's remarkable musical talent and suggested that Jaime should study with some of the best music teachers. So his parents decided to move the family to San Francisco, California.

Jaime remembers that shortly after they arrived, he went to his first **symphony** concert. He heard famous musicians giving performances. "I was in seventh heaven, and I remember being deeply moved. The violin was not forced on me in any way. I can't remember ever wanting to do anything else."

Jaime progressed quickly in his studies. When he was eight, he gave his first recital, and when he was eleven, he performed with the San Francisco Philharmonic.

A year later the family moved to Cleveland so that Jaime could study with Josef Gingold, a well-known music teacher. Jaime says that Mr. Gingold, who was like a second father to him, made his love for the violin even greater.

Before he studied with Mr. Gingold, Jaime did not like practicing **scales,** so he tried not to play them. But Mr. Gingold made the scale exercises interesting and enjoyable. Later Jaime attended the Curtis Institute in Philadelphia. There he started playing the viola.

In 1959 when Jaime was seventeen, he won first prize in a famous musical competition, and his career as a soloist began. But Jaime was not content with being a soloist; he also loved being a **chamber music** player. At that time, however, most musicians chose to be either a soloist or a chamber music player. His manager told him that if he continued playing chamber music, he would ruin his solo career. Jaime was just nineteen. He was worried about what his manager said, but he told him that chamber music had to be part of his life, too.

Now Jaime continues to work as a soloist and as part of a group. Often he plays in a trio with the pianist Joseph Kalichstein and the cellist Sharon Robinson, who is his wife. Jaime says that he loves playing both the violin and the viola at a performance because he gets to know different parts of the music.

Jaime is also well known as a conductor. This part of his career was totally unplanned. Once when he was invited to perform as a soloist in Scotland, the conductor became sick. The orchestra suggested that Jamie conduct the whole concert himself. Jaime says that he knew all of the pieces very well and decided, "This will be fun!"

As a conductor Jaime believes that you can get beautiful results when every member of the orchestra becomes truly involved in the performance. So he works closely with the musicians, asking them to make suggestions about how the music should be played. "I like featuring members of the orchestra in solo roles. It's wonderful for the audience to hear these people, and it's good for the musicians, because they should never feel that they're just there to back up a soloist."

When Jaime is not on tour, he lives part of the time in New York City and part of the time in Vermont.

· · · HELPFUL VOCABULARY · · ·

viola: a musical instrument that looks like a violin, but is a little larger and a little lower in tone

string quartet: a musical group of two violins, a viola, and a cello

symphony: a large orchestra that usually plays long musical compositions

scale: a series of musical notes going up or down in equal steps

chamber music: music written for two or more instruments with each instrument playing a different part

THINKING ABOUT WHAT YOU HAVE READ

1. How did Jaime's life change when he was five years old?

_____

2. What musical skills does Jaime have?

_____

_____

3. What are some things you learned about Jaime's parents? Give examples.

_____

_____

4. Why was Josef Gingold a good teacher?

_____

_____

5. When Jaime was first beginning his musical career, how was he different from other musicians?

_____

6. How does Jaime work with the musicians that he conducts?

_____

_____

WORKING WITH WORDS

What is Jaime Laredo like? List four adjectives that describe him.

_____   _____

_____   _____

What new words did you learn from the story?

_____   _____   _____

Use two of them in sentences.

_____

_____

Jaime Laredo has been called a "jack-of-all-trades." What do you think this means?

_____

_____

_____

Read the story again. Then fill in the bubbles in the picture with words that Jaime and his manager might have said to each other when they talked about his playing chamber music.

WRITING SKILLS

Imagine that Jaime Laredo is going to give a performance in the town or city where you live. Write a paragraph telling about Jaime Laredo for your school paper. Be sure to include a topic and a concluding sentence. Before you begin, write down three points you want to include in your report.

1. _____

2. _____

3. _____

Jamie Laredo Gives Concert in _____

_____

_____

_____

_____

_____

_____

Pretend that you are seventeen-year-old Jaime Laredo. Write a journal entry describing how you felt when you won the musical competition.

_____

_____

_____

_____

If you had a large farm, what plants would you like to grow?

_____

_____

Drawing by Hans U. Neukomm

Indigo.   H.N.

Eliza Lucas Pinckney
1722–1793

"What kind of crop can I grow that people will want to buy?" Eliza wondered. The year was 1739, and Colonel Lucas had just told his seventeen-year-old daughter that the army was sending him to Antigua, West Indies. His wife was an **invalid;** Colonel Lucas was leaving Eliza in the Carolinas to take care of her mother and three younger brothers and sisters. In addition, he wanted her to manage the family's five thousand acres.

Eliza was well prepared to do this. She had been born in Antigua, West Indies, and then educated in England. As a child she was very curious and full of energy. Eliza loved books and would often read those she found in her father's library. She spoke French, played the flute, and taught her younger brothers and sisters. But one of her greatest interests was plants and how they grew.

Before her father left, he suggested that she experiment with crops for their plantation. In the Carolinas, rice was the main crop for **export,** but bad weather conditions could completely ruin rice. The colonists needed a crop they could depend on.

After arriving in Antigua, her father sent her seeds, and Eliza tried to grow ginger, cotton, and alfalfa. In 1742, after raising several different crops, Eliza decided to try indigo, a plant that produced a beautiful dark blue dye. At that time, Montserrat, an island in the Caribbean, controlled by the French, grew indigo and supplied most of the dye used by the colonists. People thought that it was impossible to grow this plant in the Carolinas because seventy years before farmers had tried and failed. It seemed that the soil and weather conditions there were not right for it.

Eliza knew that if she was successful, she would help the colonists, who wanted to develop products they could sell to other countries. If the colonists could make this expensive blue dye at home, many countries would be interested in buying it.

Eliza found she could grow a good crop of indigo, but she had difficulty in producing the dye. The dye material had to be removed from the indigo plant, refined, and compressed into **soluble** chunks. This was a very complicated process.

Her father sent a **chemist** from Montserrat to help her. But this man was afraid that if the colonists could produce the dye, the indigo business on his own island would be harmed. So he **sabotaged** the first batch. Eliza threw him out of the house; later she hired his brother to help her.

By 1744 Eliza had learned how to produce indigo dye, and within three years she had made enough to sell to Britain. She gave most of her crop, however, to other growers in the Carolinas, so that the seeds could be planted throughout the area.

When she was twenty-two, she married Charles Pinckney, a respected lawyer in South Carolina. They had four children. Along with caring for her family, Eliza continued to manage her plantations.

Because of Eliza's work, indigo became the largest money-making crop in colonial America. President Washington admired her so much that when she died of cancer at the age of seventy-one, he asked if he could be a **pallbearer** at her funeral.

Note: A drawing of the indigo plant is used at the beginning of the story because there are no pictures of Eliza Lucas Pinckney.

· · · HELPFUL VOCABULARY · · ·

invalid: a person who is unable to take care of himself or herself because of a continuing sickness

export: to send goods to other countries to be sold or traded

soluble: able to be softened in another substance

chemist: person who works or specializes in chemistry

sabotage: to damage or destroy buildings, machinery, or other property on purpose; to interfere

pallbearer: a person who carries or walks along with the coffin at a funeral

THINKING ABOUT WHAT YOU HAVE READ

1. Why do we remember Eliza Lucas Pinckney?

_____

_____

2. What was Eliza like as a child?

_____

_____

3. In 1739 what did Colonel Lucas want Eliza to do?

_____

4. What did Colonel Lucas think of his daughter? Use examples from the story to tell why you think so.

_____

_____

_____

5. How was seventeen-year-old Eliza's life different from the lives of most seventeen-year-old girls today?

_____

_____

_____

6. Why do you think there are no pictures of Eliza Lucas Pinckney?

_____

_____

WORKING WITH WORDS

How many adjectives (describing words) can you think of that tell what Eliza was like. Try to write at least five.

_____

_____

A **category** is a group or class of things. For example, the category of trees includes pine, oak, elm, and so on. Try to list four items for each category.

states in the American south

_____

cities in the American south

_____

kinds of crops

_____

American presidents

_____

islands in the Caribbean

_____

WRITING SKILLS

Write about an experiment that you would like to perform. Explain why you want to perform it. Then draw a picture of your experiment.

_____

_____

_____

_____

A storyboard is a set of pictures that tell a story. It is often used to plan a movie. Make a storyboard telling about Eliza's life. In each box draw a picture. Show the different things Eliza did.

1

2

3

4

5

Write what is happening in each box.

1._____

2._____

3._____

4._____

5._____

LOOKING BACK

Which person in this book do you think was the most interesting?

_____

Why do you think this?

_____

_____

_____

Fifteen years from now, which person would you most like to
be like?

_____

Why do you think this?

_____

_____

_____

Now draw a picture of what you think you will be doing in fifteen years.

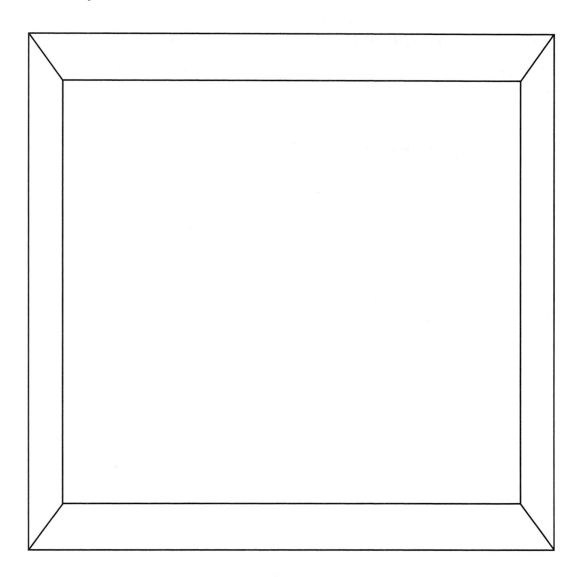

You have just finished reading stories about the lives of many different people. These are **biographies.** When a person writes a story about his or her own life, it is called an **autobiography.** Think about your life. Then try to write your autobiography.

_____

_____

_____

_____

_____

_____

_____

_____

_____

_____

_____